THE FATHERHOOD BLUEPRINT

Creating a Mastery Mindset for Fatherhood

Antonio R. Broadnax M. Ed

Copyright © 2023 Success Built on Vision Learning House Publishing.

All rights reserved.

No part of this publication may be reproduced, stored in a retrieval system, or transmitted, in any form or by any means, without the prior permission in writing of the publisher, nor be otherwise circulated in any form of binding or cover other than that in which it is published and without a similar condition being imposed on the subsequent purchaser.

This is a work of fiction. Names, characters, places, and incidents are either products of the author's imagination or are used fictitiously. Any resemblance to actual persons, living or dead, events, or locales is entirely coincidental.

Published by Success Built on Vision Learning House Publishing.

Printed in the United States of America

THE FATHERHOOD BLUEPRINT

Creating a Mastery Mindset for Fatherhood

CONTENT

Introduction 1
    Importance of a Mastery Mindset for Fatherhood 1
    Brief Summary of the Fatherhood Blueprint 3
    Overview of the book contents 4

Understanding a Mastery Mindset 7
    What is a Mastery Mindset? 7
    Characteristics of a Mastery Mindset 9
    Benefits of a Mastery Mindset for Fatherhood 11

The Fatherhood Blueprint 14
    Framework of the Fatherhood Blueprint 14
    The 5 Pillars of Fatherhood Mastery 16
    Self-awareness 19

- Mindset 21
- Communication 24
- Relationship Building 26
- Legacy 28

Self-awareness 30
- Understanding your strengths and weaknesses 30
- Identifying limiting beliefs 32
- Developing a growth mindset 34

Mindset 37
- The power of thoughts and beliefs 37
- Developing a positive mindset 41

Communication 44
- Active listening 44
- Effective communication skills 47
- Conflict resolution 49

Relationship Building 52
- Building trust and rapport 52
- Strengthening family relationships 54
- Balancing work and family 56

Legacy 59
- Creating a meaningful legacy 59

Passing on values and traditions 61

Leaving a positive impact on your family 63

Putting it All Together 65

Developing a personal action plan 65

Implementing the Fatherhood Blueprint 67

Measuring progress and success 70

Conclusion 73

The importance of a Mastery Mindset for Fatherhood 73

Reflection on the Fatherhood Blueprint 75

Final Thoughts 78

Appendix 80

Additional Resources 80

Worksheets and Exercises 82

Glossary of Terms. 87

INTRODUCTION

Importance of a Mastery Mindset for Fatherhood

Fatherhood is a journey that requires a mastery mindset. As a father, you must be willing to adopt a mindset that fosters growth, self-improvement, and excellence. A mastery mindset is an attitude that enables you to believe that you can learn, grow, and improve over time. It is a mindset that allows you to approach fatherhood with a positive attitude, an open mind, and a willingness to learn from your experiences.

The importance of a mastery mindset for fatherhood cannot be overemphasized. It is the key that unlocks your potential as a father, enables you to connect with your children, and helps you to build a strong and loving relationship with them. A mastery mindset allows you to approach fatherhood with a clear sense of purpose, a deep understanding of your strengths and weaknesses, and a willingness to work hard to achieve your goals.

When you adopt a mastery mindset, you are more likely to be patient, understanding, and compassionate with your children. You are also more likely to be a positive role model for your children, as they will see you as someone who is committed to self-improvement, growth, and excellence. This will inspire them to adopt a similar mindset and work hard to achieve their own goals.

A mastery mindset also enables you to appreciate the value of mistakes and failures. You understand that they are an essential part of the learning process and that they provide valuable feedback that can help you to improve. This mindset allows you to be more resilient in the face of challenges and setbacks, which is an essential quality for fatherhood.

In conclusion, a mastery mindset is critical for fatherhood. It enables you to approach fatherhood with a positive attitude, an open mind, and a willingness to learn and grow. It helps you to connect with your children, build a strong and loving relationship with them, and be a positive role model for them. Adopting a mastery mindset is a powerful way to unlock your potential as a father and create a meaningful and fulfilling life with your children.

Brief Summary of the Fatherhood Blueprint

The Fatherhood Blueprint is a comprehensive guide for fathers who want to develop a mastery mindset in their journey of fatherhood. The book is divided into three parts, with each section focusing on a different aspect of fatherhood.

Part 1 of the book focuses on the mindset of a mastery father. It delves into the importance of developing a positive mindset, setting goals, and taking action towards achieving those goals. The section also emphasizes the importance of self-awareness, self-regulation, and self-motivation as key factors in becoming a successful father.

Part 2 of the book discusses the role of communication in fatherhood. It highlights the importance of effective communication in building strong relationships with children, spouses, and other family members. The section also provides practical tips on how to communicate effectively, including active listening, empathy, and clarity.

Part 3 of the book focuses on the practical aspects of fatherhood. It covers topics such as discipline, parenting styles, and the importance of spending quality time with children. The section also provides practical advice on how to handle challenging situations, such as dealing with a child's tantrums or managing stress.

Overall, The Fatherhood Blueprint is an excellent resource for fathers who want to develop a mastery mindset in their journey of fatherhood. It provides a comprehensive guide on how to develop the mindset, skills, and behaviors needed to become a successful father. Whether you are a new father or a seasoned one, this book has something to offer for everyone. By following the principles outlined in the book, you can become the best father you can be and provide your children with the love, support, and guidance they need to thrive.

Overview of the book contents

The Fatherhood Blueprint: Creating a Mastery Mindset for Fatherhood is a book that aims to help fathers develop a mindset that enables them to master their roles as fathers. The book is divided into three sections, each exploring different aspects of fatherhood and the mastery mindset.

In the first section, the book delves into the importance of having a mastery mindset and the benefits it brings to fatherhood. It explores the challenges that fathers face in modern society and how a mastery mindset can help them overcome these challenges. The section also highlights the key principles of the mastery mindset, including self-awareness, resilience, and adaptability.

The second section of the book focuses on the practical aspects of fatherhood. It covers topics such as effective communication with children, setting boundaries, and managing conflicts. The section also explores the importance of being present in a child's life and the impact it has on their growth and development.

The final section of the book looks at the bigger picture of fatherhood and its impact on society. It explores the role of fathers in shaping the future generation and the responsibility that comes with it. The section also highlights the importance of building a supportive community of fathers who can learn from each other's experiences and help each other grow.

Throughout the book, readers will find practical tips, real-life examples, and exercises that will help them develop a mastery mindset for fatherhood. The book is aimed at fathers who want to become better fathers, and those who are already doing a great job but want to take their parenting skills to the next level.

In summary, The Fatherhood Blueprint: Creating a Mastery Mindset for Fatherhood is a comprehensive guide that provides a roadmap for fathers to develop a mastery mindset that will enable them to be the best fathers they can be. The book is a must-read for any father who wants to take their parenting skills to the next level and make a positive impact on their children's lives.

UNDERSTANDING A MASTERY MINDSET

What is a Mastery Mindset?

The Mastery Mindset is a way of thinking that enables individuals to achieve their desired outcomes by developing a set of skills and beliefs that help them overcome obstacles and challenges. In the context of fatherhood, a Mastery Mindset means adopting a proactive approach to parenting and committing oneself to continuous improvement.

A Mastery Mindset involves setting clear goals and developing a plan to achieve them. It requires asking oneself what kind of father one wants to be and outlining the steps needed to get there. A Mastery Mindset also involves being open to feedback and using failures as opportunities to learn and grow.

Fathers with a Mastery Mindset are mindful of their parenting styles and are intentional in their interactions with their children. They understand that their words and actions have a significant impact on their children's development and strive to be positive role models.

Moreover, fathers with a Mastery Mindset prioritize their physical and mental health. They recognize the importance of self-care and make time for activities that promote their well-being. They also understand that taking care of themselves enables them to be better fathers.

A Mastery Mindset also involves being adaptable and resilient. Fathers with this mindset understand that parenting is an ever-changing journey, and they are willing to adjust their approach as their children grow and develop. They are also prepared to face challenges and setbacks and use them as opportunities to learn and grow.

In summary, adopting a Mastery Mindset is essential for fathers who want to be intentional in their parenting and create a fulfilling relationship with their children. It involves setting clear goals, being mindful of one's parenting style, prioritizing self-care, and being adaptable and resilient. By embracing this mindset, fathers can create a legacy of positive influence that will impact their children for years to come.

Characteristics of a Mastery Mindset

A mastery mindset is essential for fathers who wish to be successful in their journey of fatherhood. It is a mindset that empowers fathers to maintain their focus, stay motivated, and remain persistent in the pursuit of their goals. It helps fathers to overcome challenges, learn from their mistakes, and achieve their full potential. In this subchapter, we will explore the characteristics of a mastery mindset and how fathers can cultivate this mindset to become better fathers.

The first characteristic of a mastery mindset is the belief that success is achievable. This belief is crucial because it drives fathers to take action and pursue their goals with determination. Fathers with a mastery mindset understand that success is not easy, but it is possible with hard work, persistence, and dedication. They are not deterred by setbacks, failures, or obstacles because they understand that these are part of the learning process.

The second characteristic of a mastery mindset is the desire for continuous learning and improvement. Fathers with a mastery mindset are always looking for ways to improve their knowledge, skills, and abilities. They are open to feedback, willing to learn from their mistakes, and constantly seeking new challenges to push themselves to their limits. They understand that growth is a lifelong process and are committed to self-improvement.

The third characteristic of a mastery mindset is resilience. Fathers with a mastery mindset are resilient in the face of adversity. They have a strong sense of purpose and are committed to their goals, even when faced with challenges. They are able to bounce back from setbacks and failures, learn from their experiences, and move forward with renewed energy and determination.

The fourth characteristic of a mastery mindset is a focus on the process rather than the outcome. Fathers with a mastery mindset focus on the journey rather than the destination. They understand that success is not just about achieving a particular goal but also about the journey of self-discovery and personal growth. They enjoy the process of learning, growing, and improving, and are not solely driven by the end result.

In conclusion, cultivating a mastery mindset is essential for fathers who wish to be successful in their journey of fatherhood. Fathers with a mastery mindset believe that success is achievable, have a desire for continuous learning and improvement, are resilient in the face of adversity, and focus on the process rather than the outcome. By adopting these characteristics, fathers can become better fathers and achieve their full potential in all areas of their lives.

Benefits of a Mastery Mindset for Fatherhood

As fathers, we all want to be the best we can be for our families. We want to provide for them, protect them, and guide them through life. But how do we become the best fathers possible? The answer lies in developing a mastery mindset.

A mastery mindset is a way of thinking that allows us to continuously improve ourselves and our skills. When we adopt a mastery mindset, we see challenges as opportunities to learn and grow, rather than obstacles to be avoided. This mindset not only benefits us in our personal and professional lives, but it can also have a profound impact on our role as fathers.

Here are some of the benefits of a mastery mindset for fatherhood:

1. Improved Communication: When we adopt a mastery mindset, we become better listeners and communicators. We learn to ask questions, seek feedback, and communicate our thoughts and feelings in a clear and concise manner. This allows us to build stronger relationships with our children and better understand their needs and desires.

2. Increased Patience: Fatherhood can be challenging at times, and it's easy to become frustrated or overwhelmed. But when we adopt a mastery mindset, we learn to embrace challenges and view them as opportunities for growth. This helps us to be more patient and understanding with our children, even during difficult times.

3. Better Time Management: As fathers, we often have a lot on our plates. We have to balance work, family, and other responsibilities. But when we adopt a mastery mindset, we learn to prioritize our time and focus on the things that matter most. This allows us to be more efficient and effective in our roles as fathers.

4. Increased Confidence: When we develop a mastery mindset, we become more confident in our abilities as fathers. We trust ourselves to make the right decisions and take action when needed. This confidence not only benefits us, but it also helps to instill confidence in our children.

5. Improved Problem-Solving Skills: Fatherhood is full of challenges and obstacles. But when we adopt a mastery mindset, we learn to approach these challenges with a problem-solving mindset. We focus on finding solutions rather than dwelling on the problem itself. This helps us to be more effective in our role as fathers and teaches our children valuable problem-solving skills.

In conclusion, developing a mastery mindset is an essential component of being a successful father. By adopting this mindset, we can improve our communication, increase our patience, better manage our time, increase our confidence, and improve our problem-solving skills. These benefits not only benefit us as fathers, but they also have a positive impact on our children's lives.

THE FATHERHOOD BLUEPRINT

Framework of the Fatherhood Blueprint

The Fatherhood Blueprint provides a comprehensive guide to mastering the art of fatherhood. The framework of the Fatherhood Blueprint is a critical aspect of the book, and it outlines the essential steps that fathers can take to create a mastery mindset for fatherhood.

The first step in the framework of the Fatherhood Blueprint is to set clear and specific goals. These goals should be challenging, yet achievable, and should be focused on the long-term development of your child. By setting goals, fathers can create a clear path to success and can measure progress along the way.

The second step is to develop a growth mindset. This involves embracing challenges, learning from mistakes, and persisting in the face of adversity. Fathers with a growth mindset are more likely to take risks, try new things, and push themselves to be the best father possible.

The third step is to create a positive and supportive environment for your child. This involves modeling positive behaviors, providing emotional support, and creating a sense of safety and security for your child. Fathers who create a positive environment help their children to thrive and achieve their full potential.

The fourth step is to establish clear boundaries and expectations. This involves setting rules and consequences, communicating them clearly to your child, and following through consistently. Fathers who establish clear boundaries and expectations help their children to develop self-discipline and make better choices.

The fifth and final step is to prioritize self-care. This involves taking care of your physical, emotional, and mental health, so you can be the best father possible. Fathers who prioritize self-care are better able to manage stress, stay focused on their goals, and maintain healthy relationships with their children and family.

In conclusion, the framework of the Fatherhood Blueprint provides a roadmap for fathers to create a mastery mindset for fatherhood. By setting goals, developing a growth mindset, creating a positive environment, establishing clear boundaries and expectations, and prioritizing self-care, fathers can become the best possible role models and mentors for their children.

The 5 Pillars of Fatherhood Mastery

Fatherhood is an incredible journey that requires a lot of effort, patience, and dedication. As a father, your role is not only to provide for your family but also to be a mentor, a guide, and a role model to your children. To achieve this, you need to develop a Mastery Mindset for Fatherhood. A Mastery Mindset is a mindset that enables you to take control of your life, overcome challenges, and achieve your goals. In this chapter, we will discuss the five pillars of Fatherhood Mastery.

1. Self-Awareness

The first pillar of Fatherhood Mastery is self-awareness. This means being aware of your strengths, weaknesses, values, and beliefs. Self-awareness enables you to understand your emotions, feelings, and behaviors. It also helps you to identify areas in your life that need improvement. By being self-aware, you can become a better father by understanding your children's needs, communicating effectively with them, and setting a good example for them.

2. Emotional Intelligence

The second pillar of Fatherhood Mastery is emotional intelligence. Emotional intelligence is the ability to recognize, understand, and manage your emotions and the emotions of others. As a father, emotional intelligence enables you to connect with your children, empathize with them, and respond appropriately to their needs. Emotional intelligence also helps you to manage stress, conflicts, and challenges in your family.

3. Communication

The third pillar of Fatherhood Mastery is communication. Communication is the key to building strong relationships with your children. Effective communication involves listening actively, expressing yourself clearly, and being respectful of others' opinions. As a father, communication enables you to understand your children's perspectives, share your own thoughts and feelings with them, and resolve conflicts.

4. Time Management

The fourth pillar of Fatherhood Mastery is time management. Time management is the ability to use your time effectively and efficiently. As a father, time management enables you to balance your work and family responsibilities, prioritize your tasks, and spend quality time with your children. Time management also helps you to avoid burnout and maintain a healthy work-life balance.

5. Continuous Learning

The fifth pillar of Fatherhood Mastery is continuous learning. Continuous learning involves acquiring new knowledge, skills, and experiences that enable you to grow as a father. As a father, continuous learning enables you to stay updated on the latest parenting trends, understand your children's developmental stages, and improve your parenting skills.

In conclusion, the five pillars of Fatherhood Mastery are self-awareness, emotional intelligence, communication, time management, and continuous learning. By mastering these pillars, you can become a better father and create a fulfilling and meaningful life for yourself and your family. Remember, fatherhood is a journey, and with a Mastery Mindset, you can make the most of it.

Self-awareness

Self-awareness is the cornerstone of creating a mastery mindset for fatherhood. It is the ability to understand your own emotions, thoughts, and behavior, and how they impact your relationships with your children, partner, and others in your life. Self-awareness is essential for effective parenting because it helps you recognize your strengths and weaknesses, identify areas for improvement, and make conscious decisions that align with your values and goals.

As a father, you may have learned certain patterns of behavior and communication from your own upbringing that you unconsciously repeat in your interactions with your children. Self-awareness helps you break free from these patterns and develop a more intentional and mindful approach to parenting. It allows you to be present and fully engaged with your children, rather than being reactive or distracted by your own internal dialogue.

Self-awareness also involves cultivating a non-judgmental attitude towards yourself. It means accepting your imperfections and mistakes, and being compassionate and forgiving towards yourself when you fall short of your own expectations. This mindset frees you from the burden of self-criticism and guilt, and enables you to model self-compassion and empathy for your children.

To develop your self-awareness, it is helpful to practice mindfulness and reflection. Mindfulness involves paying attention to your thoughts, emotions, and sensations in the present moment, without judgment or distraction. You can incorporate mindfulness into your daily routine by taking a few moments to breathe deeply and focus on your senses, or by engaging in activities that bring you joy and relaxation.

Reflection involves taking time to review your interactions with your children and identify patterns or triggers that may be affecting your behavior. You can journal about your thoughts and feelings, or discuss them with a trusted friend or therapist. By reflecting on your experiences, you can gain insight into your own strengths and weaknesses as a father, and develop strategies to enhance your parenting skills.

In conclusion, self-awareness is an essential component of creating a mastery mindset for fatherhood. By cultivating mindfulness and reflection, you can develop a deeper understanding of yourself and your parenting style, and become more intentional and compassionate in your interactions with your children.

Mindset

As a father, your mindset is crucial in determining the quality of your fatherhood experience. Your mindset is the set of beliefs, attitudes, and values that you hold about yourself, your children, and your role as a father. It influences how you perceive and respond to situations, people, and challenges that you encounter as a father.

A mastery mindset is the key to achieving your full potential as a father. It is a mindset that focuses on continuous learning, growth, and improvement. It enables you to approach fatherhood with a sense of purpose, passion, and resilience. Here are some tips on how to cultivate a mastery mindset as a father.

1. Adopt a growth mindset

A growth mindset is the belief that your abilities and intelligence can be developed through hard work, dedication, and perseverance. It is the opposite of a fixed mindset, which assumes that your abilities and intelligence are fixed traits that cannot be changed. By adopting a growth mindset, you can approach fatherhood as a learning experience, where you can continuously improve and develop your skills and abilities.

2. Set goals

Goal setting is a powerful tool for achieving success in any area of life, including fatherhood. By setting specific, measurable, achievable, relevant, and time-bound (SMART) goals, you can focus your efforts and energy on achieving meaningful outcomes. Your goals should align with your values, vision, and priorities as a father.

3. Develop a positive attitude

A positive attitude is essential for maintaining a mastery mindset. It involves focusing on the good things in life, cultivating gratitude, and reframing negative situations in a positive light. By developing a positive attitude, you can approach fatherhood with optimism, enthusiasm, and resilience.

4. Embrace challenges

Challenges are opportunities for growth and learning. By embracing challenges, you can develop your skills, overcome obstacles, and build resilience. As a father, you will encounter many challenges, from dealing with tantrums to managing finances. By approaching these challenges with a growth mindset and a positive attitude, you can turn them into opportunities for growth and learning.

5. Seek feedback

Feedback is essential for growth and improvement. By seeking feedback from your children, your partner, and other trusted sources, you can gain insights into your strengths and weaknesses as a father. This feedback can help you identify areas for improvement, refine your goals, and develop your skills and abilities.

In conclusion, cultivating a mastery mindset is the key to achieving your full potential as a father. It involves adopting a growth mindset, setting goals, developing a positive attitude, embracing challenges, and seeking feedback. By applying these principles, you can approach fatherhood with purpose, passion, and resilience, and create a meaningful and fulfilling fatherhood experience.

Communication

Communication is a vital aspect of fatherhood. It is how you express your love, share your values, and build a strong relationship with your children. Effective communication is crucial in developing a mastery mindset for fatherhood. It helps you to be more present, understanding, and empathetic towards your children.

Communication is more than just talking. It is about actively listening, understanding, and being attentive to your children's needs. As a father, you need to create an environment that promotes open communication. Encourage your children to express their thoughts and feelings without fear of judgment or ridicule. This will help you to understand them better and provide the necessary support and guidance.

One of the most important aspects of communication is being present. In today's world, it is easy to get distracted by phones, work, and other things. However, when you are with your children, make a conscious effort to be present.

Put away your phone, turn off the TV, and focus on them. This will help you to connect with them on a deeper level and build a stronger bond.

When communicating with your children, it is essential to be empathetic. Put yourself in their shoes and try to understand their perspective. This will help you to respond in a way that is compassionate and supportive. Remember, your children look up to you, and how you communicate with them will shape their understanding of the world around them.

Another critical aspect of communication is setting boundaries. As a father, you need to establish clear boundaries with your children. This will help them to understand what is expected of them and what is not acceptable. Setting boundaries will also help you to maintain a healthy relationship with your children and avoid conflicts.

In conclusion, effective communication is an essential component of fatherhood. It helps you to build a strong relationship with your children, understand their needs, and provide the necessary support and guidance. By being present, empathetic, and setting boundaries, you can create an environment that fosters open communication and promotes a mastery mindset for fatherhood.

Relationship Building

Relationship building is a crucial aspect of fatherhood. Being a father is not just about providing financial support to your children; it is also about building strong relationships with them. Your children need to know that they are loved, valued, and appreciated. This can only be achieved through intentional relationship building.

One of the best ways to build relationships with your children is by spending quality time with them. You should make it a priority to set aside time to spend with your kids, whether it is playing games, going on outings, or simply having conversations with them. By doing this, you are showing your children that you value them and that they are important to you.

Another essential aspect of relationship building is effective communication. As a father, you should create an open and safe environment for your children to express themselves. You should listen to their thoughts, opinions, and feelings without judgment. This will help you understand your children better and build a deeper connection with them.

Showing affection is another critical component of relationship building. Hugging, kissing, and saying "I love you" can go a long way in making your children feel loved and appreciated. It is important to note that children have different love languages, and you should strive to understand your child's love language and express your affection in ways that resonate with them.

In addition to building relationships with your children, you should also invest in your relationship with your partner. A strong and healthy romantic relationship can positively impact your children's emotional well-being. You should make time to connect with your partner and work through any challenges that may arise.

In conclusion, relationship building is a critical aspect of fatherhood. By spending quality time with your children, effective communication, showing affection, and investing in your romantic relationship, you can create a strong foundation for a healthy and fulfilling family dynamic.

Legacy

Legacy

As a father, one of the most important things you can do is to leave a lasting legacy for your children. This is not just about leaving them a financial inheritance or a material legacy, but also about leaving behind a set of values, beliefs, and principles that they can carry with them throughout their lives.

Your legacy as a father is not just about what you do, but also about who you are. Your children will learn more from your actions than from your words, so it is important to live your life with integrity and to model the kind of behavior that you want your children to emulate.

One of the keys to leaving a positive legacy for your children is to focus on building strong relationships with them. This means spending quality time with them, listening to them, and showing them that you care about their thoughts, feelings, and opinions. When your children feel valued and loved, they are more likely to internalize the values and principles that you want to pass on to them.

Another important aspect of leaving a legacy for your children is to be intentional about the kind of values and principles that you want to instill in them. This means taking the time to reflect on what is truly important to you and then actively working to pass those values on to your children.

For example, if you believe that honesty and integrity are important, then you need to model these traits in your own life and actively teach your children about the importance of telling the truth and doing the right thing, even when it is difficult.

Ultimately, your legacy as a father is about creating a sense of purpose, meaning, and direction for your children. By instilling the right values and principles in them, you can help them to become the kind of people who will make a positive difference in the world.

In order to leave a lasting legacy for your children, it is important to be intentional, to model the behavior that you want to see in them, and to build strong relationships with them. By doing these things, you can create a powerful legacy that will impact your children for generations to come.

SELF-AWARENESS

Understanding your strengths and weaknesses

Understanding your strengths and weaknesses is a crucial aspect of developing a mastery mindset as a father. Mastery mindset is all about becoming the best version of yourself, and this starts with knowing yourself inside out. As a father, you need to identify your strengths and weaknesses to become more effective in your role.

Strengths can be defined as your innate abilities or talents that come naturally to you. These are the things that you excel at, enjoy doing, and that give you a sense of accomplishment. Some fathers may have strengths in communication, problem-solving, leadership, or even cooking. Knowing your strengths helps you to leverage them and use them to your advantage in your fatherhood journey.

On the other hand, weaknesses are areas where you struggle or find challenging. These could be behaviors, habits, or skills that you need to improve or develop. For instance, some fathers may struggle with time management, emotional regulation, or managing finances. Identifying your weaknesses is the first step towards improving them and becoming a better father.

One of the most effective ways to identify your strengths and weaknesses is through self-reflection. Take time to think about your past experiences, successes, and failures. Ask yourself what you did right and what you could have done better. Also, seek feedback from other people, especially those who know you well, such as your partner, family, or close friends.

Once you have identified your strengths and weaknesses, the next step is to create a plan to improve them. For your strengths, think about how you can use them more effectively in your fatherhood journey. For your weaknesses, think about the specific actions you can take to improve them. This could be through learning, seeking advice or support, or practicing new behaviors.

In conclusion, understanding your strengths and weaknesses is an essential aspect of developing a mastery mindset as a father. Knowing yourself inside out helps you become more effective in your role and ultimately become the best father you can be.

Identifying limiting beliefs

Identifying Limiting Beliefs

As fathers, we often hold limiting beliefs that can hold us back from achieving our goals and being the best dads we can be. These beliefs are often deeply ingrained in our subconscious and can be difficult to identify. However, it is essential to recognize them and address them if we want to create a mastery mindset for fatherhood.

Limiting beliefs are beliefs that hold us back from achieving our full potential. They can be related to our abilities, personality, or even our circumstances. For example, a father may believe that he is not a patient person and therefore can never be a good dad. This belief can hold him back from developing his patience and becoming a better father.

To identify limiting beliefs, we need to become aware of the thoughts and feelings that hold us back. We can do this by paying attention to our self-talk and emotions. When we notice negative self-talk or feelings of self-doubt, we can ask ourselves what beliefs are behind them.

Another way to identify limiting beliefs is to look at our past experiences. Often, our beliefs are formed based on past experiences, and we may continue to hold onto them even if they no longer serve us. For example, a father who grew up in a household where emotions were not expressed may believe that showing emotions is a sign of weakness. This belief can hold him back from connecting with his children emotionally.

Once we have identified our limiting beliefs, we can begin to challenge them. We can ask ourselves if they are true and if they serve us. If they are not true or do not serve us, we can replace them with more empowering beliefs. For example, the father who believes he is not patient can replace that belief with the belief that he can develop his patience with practice.

Identifying and addressing limiting beliefs is a crucial step in creating a mastery mindset for fatherhood. By doing so, we can overcome the barriers that hold us back and become the best dads we can be.

Developing a growth mindset

Developing a Growth Mindset

As a father, you are likely to have a lot of responsibilities and challenges that come with parenting. Some of these challenges may seem difficult or even impossible to overcome, but with the right mindset, you can develop the skills and strategies to handle them with ease.

One of the most important mindsets to cultivate as a father is a growth mindset. A growth mindset is the belief that your abilities can be developed and improved through hard work and dedication. This mindset is essential for achieving success in any area of your life, including fatherhood.

Here are some tips for developing a growth mindset as a father:

1. Embrace Challenges

When faced with a challenge, many people tend to shy away or give up. However, in order to develop a growth mindset, you need to embrace challenges as opportunities for growth and learning. Instead of seeing challenges as obstacles, see them as chances to develop new skills and strategies.

2. Learn from Failure

Failure is a natural part of the learning process. Instead of beating yourself up over a failure or setback, use it as an opportunity to learn and grow. Ask yourself what you can do differently next time and use that knowledge to improve your future outcomes.

3. Believe in Yourself

Believing in yourself is essential for developing a growth mindset. When you believe that you are capable of achieving your goals, you are more likely to take risks and pursue opportunities. Even if you don't feel confident at first, practice self-affirmations and visualize yourself succeeding.

4. Seek Feedback

Feedback is essential for growth and improvement. Seek out feedback from your partner, your children, and other trusted sources. Use that feedback to identify areas where you can improve and develop new skills.

5. Keep Learning

Finally, keep learning and developing new skills. Read books, attend workshops, and seek out mentors who can help you grow as a father. By continually learning and developing new skills, you can achieve a growth mindset that will help you succeed in all areas of your life.

In conclusion, developing a growth mindset is essential for succeeding as a father. Embrace challenges, learn from failure, believe in yourself, seek feedback, and keep learning. With these strategies, you can cultivate a mindset that will help you achieve mastery in fatherhood and in life.

MINDSET

The power of thoughts and beliefs

The power of thoughts and beliefs is a force that shapes our lives, from the way we perceive ourselves to the way we interact with the world around us. As fathers, the way we think and the beliefs we hold can significantly impact our ability to create a successful and fulfilling life for ourselves and our families.

Our thoughts and beliefs are like seeds that we plant in our minds. These seeds grow and manifest in our lives, shaping our actions, decisions, and habits. For example, if we believe that we are not good enough or capable enough, we may find ourselves constantly doubting our abilities and not living up to our full potential as fathers and as individuals.

On the other hand, if we believe in ourselves and our abilities, we are more likely to take risks, pursue our dreams, and create a life that aligns with our values and passions.

As fathers, it is crucial to cultivate a positive and growth-oriented mindset. This means challenging negative self-talk and limiting beliefs that hold us back and replacing them with empowering and affirming thoughts.

One way to do this is to practice gratitude and focus on the good in our lives. When we shift our attention to the positive aspects of our lives, we are more likely to see opportunities and possibilities that we may have missed otherwise.

Additionally, setting goals and visualizing our success can help us to create a powerful and unstoppable mindset. By envisioning our ideal future and taking action towards it, we can build confidence and a sense of purpose that propels us forward.

Ultimately, the power of thoughts and beliefs lies in our ability to shape our reality. As fathers, we have the opportunity to create a life that is full of joy, purpose, and fulfillment by cultivating a mastery mindset that empowers us to live our best lives.

Changing negative thought patterns

As fathers, we can sometimes fall into the trap of negative thought patterns, which can lead to frustration, stress, and ultimately, a lack of fulfillment in our role as dads. However, changing negative thought patterns can be a powerful tool in enhancing our mastery mindset for fatherhood.

Negative thought patterns can manifest in different ways; from self-doubt, negative self-talk, to pessimism, and procrastination. When these thoughts take hold, they can impact our performance as dads by affecting our confidence, motivation, and ability to connect with our children.

To change negative thought patterns and develop a mastery mindset for fatherhood, we need to start by identifying our negative thoughts. This involves becoming more aware of our internal dialogue and the impact it has on our emotions, actions, and behavior.

Once we have identified our negative thoughts, we can challenge them by asking ourselves whether they are true, helpful, and relevant to the situation at hand. For instance, if we catch ourselves thinking, "I am a terrible dad," we can challenge that thought by questioning whether it's true or whether we have evidence to support it. We can also ask ourselves whether that thought is helpful in improving our relationship with our children or whether it's hindering our progress.

Another way to change negative thought patterns is by reframing them in a positive light. For instance, instead of thinking, "I can't handle this situation," we can reframe that thought to, "I may not know what to do right now, but I can learn and grow from this experience."

Additionally, practicing mindfulness can help us change negative thought patterns by bringing our attention to the present moment and focusing on positive thoughts and emotions. We can also cultivate positive self-talk through affirmations and visualizations, which can help us develop a more positive mindset and boost our confidence as dads.

In conclusion, changing negative thought patterns is a critical step in developing a mastery mindset for fatherhood. By becoming more aware of our negative thoughts, challenging them, reframing them, and cultivating positive self-talk, we can enhance our performance as dads, strengthen our relationships with our children, and ultimately, lead a more fulfilling and rewarding life as fathers.

Developing a positive mindset

Developing a Positive Mindset

As fathers, we often face challenges and obstacles that can test our resolve and ability to stay positive. Whether it's dealing with a difficult child, managing stress at work, or navigating the ups and downs of relationships, maintaining a positive mindset is critical to our success as fathers.

But what exactly is a positive mindset, and how do we develop one? At its core, a positive mindset is an optimistic outlook on life, where we focus on the good rather than the bad, and approach challenges with a can-do attitude. It's not about ignoring the negative, but rather, choosing to see the positive in spite of it.

So how can we develop a positive mindset? Here are a few tips:

1. Practice gratitude: One of the most effective ways to cultivate a positive mindset is to practice gratitude. Take time each day to reflect on the

things you're grateful for, whether it's your health, your family, your job, or something as simple as a beautiful sunset. Focusing on the good in your life can help shift your perspective and create a more positive outlook.

2. Seek out positive influences: Surround yourself with people who inspire and uplift you. Seek out mentors, friends, or colleagues who have a positive mindset and can help you stay motivated and focused on your goals.

3. Practice mindfulness: Mindfulness is the practice of being present in the moment, without judgment or distraction. By practicing mindfulness, we can learn to let go of negative thoughts and emotions, and focus on the present moment. This can help us develop a more positive outlook and approach challenges with a clear mind.

4. Celebrate small wins: It's easy to get caught up in the big picture and overlook the small wins along the way. Take time to celebrate your successes, no matter how small they may seem. This can help build momentum and keep you motivated to achieve your goals.

5. Embrace failure: Failure is a natural part of the learning process, and it's important to embrace it rather than fear it. By viewing failure as an opportunity to learn and grow, we can develop a more positive mindset and approach challenges with a sense of curiosity and openness.

Developing a positive mindset takes time and effort, but it's a critical component of mastering fatherhood. By focusing on gratitude, seeking out positive influences, practicing mindfulness, celebrating small wins, and embracing failure, we can cultivate a positive mindset that will help us navigate the challenges of fatherhood with grace and resilience.

COMMUNICATION

Active listening

Active Listening: The Key to Building Strong Relationships with Your Kids

As a father, one of the most important skills you can develop is active listening. This means giving your full attention to your child when they are speaking to you, allowing them to express themselves fully and openly, and showing that you are genuinely interested in what they have to say.

Active listening is the foundation of good communication, and it can help you build strong, trusting relationships with your kids. When you listen actively, you create a safe space for your child to share their thoughts, feelings, and concerns. This, in turn, can help you better understand your child's perspective and help you respond in a way that is supportive and empowering.

Here are a few tips to help you develop your active listening skills:

1. Put Away Distractions

When you are talking to your child, put away your phone, turn off the TV, and focus solely on the conversation at hand. This shows your child that you value their time and that you are fully present with them.

2. Make Eye Contact

Maintaining eye contact is a powerful way to show your child that you are engaged in the conversation. It also helps you pick up on nonverbal cues, such as facial expressions and body language, which can help you better understand your child's emotions.

3. Mirror Your Child's Feelings

When your child expresses a feeling, repeat it back to them in your own words. This shows that you are listening and that you understand how they are feeling. For example, if your child says, "I'm really upset about what happened at school today," you might respond by saying, "I can see that you're feeling really upset. Would you like to talk more about what happened?"

4. Ask Open-Ended Questions

Open-ended questions encourage your child to share more about their thoughts and feelings. Instead of asking, "Did you have a good day at school?" try asking, "What was the best thing that happened at school today?" This can lead to a more meaningful conversation and help you better understand your child's experiences.

5. Validate Your Child's Feelings

Even if you don't agree with your child's perspective, it's important to validate their feelings. This shows that you respect their opinions and that you are willing to listen to them. For example, if your child says, "I hate my teacher," you might respond by saying, "It sounds like you're really frustrated with your teacher. Can you tell me more about why you feel that way?"

Active listening takes practice, but it is an essential skill for any father who wants to build strong, healthy relationships with their kids. By putting away distractions, making eye contact, mirroring your child's feelings, asking open-ended questions, and validating their feelings, you can create a safe and supportive environment for your child to express themselves fully and openly.

Effective communication skills

Effective communication skills are essential in any aspect of life, but they are particularly important in fatherhood. Being a father requires strong communication skills to build and maintain healthy relationships with your children, partner, and other family members. Effective communication is not just about talking but also about listening, understanding, and responding appropriately.

One of the most important aspects of effective communication is active listening. Active listening means being fully present and attentive to what the other person is saying. It involves giving your full attention, asking questions, and reflecting back what you have heard. When you actively listen to your children, you show them that you value their thoughts and feelings, which can help build a strong bond of trust and respect.

Another key element of effective communication is being clear and concise. As a father, you need to be able to communicate your expectations, rules, and boundaries effectively. This means using clear language, avoiding jargon, and being consistent in your messaging. When you communicate clearly, your children will be more likely to understand and follow your rules and expectations.

It is also important to be empathetic and understanding in your communication. Being empathetic means putting yourself in your children's shoes and trying to understand their perspective. This can help you communicate in a way that is more meaningful and respectful. When you show empathy, you demonstrate that you care about your children's feelings and are willing to listen to their concerns.

Finally, effective communication requires patience and practice. It takes time to develop strong communication skills, and it requires constant effort and practice. As a father, you will encounter many challenging situations that require effective communication skills. By practicing active listening, clear communication, empathy, and patience, you can improve your communication skills and become a more effective father.

In summary, effective communication skills are essential for fathers who want to develop a mastery mindset for fatherhood. By practicing active listening, clear communication, empathy, and patience, fathers can build strong relationships with their children, partners, and other family members. With practice and dedication, fathers can become effective communicators and role models for their children.

Conflict resolution

Conflict resolution is a crucial aspect of fatherhood that cannot be overlooked. As a father, you are bound to encounter conflicts in your relationships with your children, spouse, and other family members. But how you handle these conflicts can make all the difference in the world. In this subchapter, we will discuss some essential strategies for conflict resolution that will help you maintain healthy relationships with your loved ones.

The first step in conflict resolution is to understand the root cause of the problem. Many conflicts arise from miscommunication, misunderstandings, or unmet expectations. Therefore, it is crucial to take the time to listen to the other person's perspective and try to understand their point of view. When you approach conflicts with an open mind and a willingness to understand, you are more likely to find a mutually beneficial solution.

The next step is to communicate your own needs and concerns clearly and respectfully. Avoid using accusatory language or attacking the other person's character. Instead, focus on the issue at hand and express your feelings in a non-judgmental way. When you communicate your needs clearly, you give the other person a chance to understand your perspective and work towards a solution.

Another key strategy for conflict resolution is to find common ground. Even if you and the other person have different opinions or values, there may be some shared goals or interests that you can build upon. By focusing on these commonalities, you can work together towards a solution that benefits everyone involved.

Finally, it is essential to be willing to compromise. Sometimes, conflict resolution requires that both parties give a little. It may not be possible to get everything you want, but by finding a middle ground, you can reach a solution that meets everyone's needs to some degree.

In conclusion, conflict resolution is an essential skill for fathers who want to maintain healthy relationships with their loved ones. By understanding the root cause of conflicts, communicating clearly and respectfully, finding common ground, and being willing to compromise, you can resolve conflicts in a way that benefits everyone involved. Remember, conflict is inevitable, but how you handle it can make all the difference in the world.

RELATIONSHIP BUILDING

Building trust and rapport

Building Trust and Rapport

As a father, building trust and rapport with your child is essential to creating a strong bond that will last a lifetime. Trust is the foundation of any relationship, and it is especially important in the relationship between a father and his child. When you build trust and rapport with your child, you create a safe and nurturing environment where your child can thrive.

Trust is built over time through consistent actions and behaviors. Your child needs to know that they can rely on you and that you will be there for them when they need you. This means being dependable, keeping your promises, and following through on your commitments. When you show your child that you are trustworthy, they will be more likely to open up to you and share their thoughts and feelings.

Rapport, on the other hand, is built through communication and shared experiences. You need to take the time to get to know your child and understand their interests and passions. This means spending quality time with them, listening to them, and showing an interest in their lives. When you build rapport with your child, you create a connection that goes beyond the surface level.

To build trust and rapport with your child, it is important to be present and engaged in their lives. This means putting down your phone, turning off the TV, and focusing on your child when you are together. It also means being patient and understanding when your child makes mistakes or struggles with something. By showing empathy and compassion, you create an environment where your child feels safe to be themselves.

It is also important to remember that building trust and rapport is an ongoing process. It requires consistent effort and attention, and it is something that needs to be nurtured over time. By making a conscious effort to build trust and rapport with your child, you are laying the foundation for a strong and lasting relationship that will benefit both of you for years to come.

Strengthening family relationships

Family is the most significant and essential component of our lives, and the relationships we share with our family members are irreplaceable. As fathers, we have a critical role to play in strengthening and nurturing these relationships, which can have a profound impact on the well-being and happiness of our entire family.

One of the most effective ways to strengthen family relationships is through effective communication. Communication is the foundation of any strong relationship, and it is essential to be open, honest, and transparent with our family members. Encourage your children to share their thoughts, feelings, and concerns with you, and be an active listener. By being present and attentive, you can build trust and foster deeper connections with your loved ones.

Another way to strengthen family relationships is to prioritize quality time together. In today's fast-paced world, it can be challenging to find time to spend with our families. However, it is crucial to make the effort to carve out time to do things together, whether it's going on a hike, playing a board game, or simply having a family dinner. These small moments can create lasting memories and strengthen the bonds between family members.

As fathers, we must also model positive behaviors and attitudes for our children. Children learn by example, and we must set the standard for how we treat others, how we communicate, and how we handle conflicts. By demonstrating respect, empathy, and kindness, we can create a positive and supportive environment for our families.

Finally, it is essential to be patient and understanding with our family members. No family is perfect, and conflicts and disagreements will inevitably arise. However, by approaching these situations with patience, empathy, and a willingness to listen, we can work through these challenges and emerge stronger as a family.

In conclusion, strengthening family relationships is crucial to creating a happy and healthy home environment. By prioritizing communication, quality time, positive behaviors, and patience, we can build deeper connections with our loved ones and create a strong foundation for our families. As fathers, we have a critical role to play in this process, and by adopting a mastery mindset, we can become the best possible versions of ourselves for our families.

Balancing work and family

As a father, balancing work and family is one of the most challenging aspects of fatherhood. With the pressures of work and the responsibilities of being a parent, it can be difficult to find a balance between the two. However, it is essential to maintain this balance to ensure that you are able to fulfill your responsibilities both at work and at home.

The first step to balancing work and family is to establish clear boundaries between the two. This means setting specific times for work and family time and sticking to them. It is important to prioritize your family time and ensure that you are fully present during this time. This may mean turning off your phone or email notifications during family time and focusing solely on your family.

Another important aspect of balancing work and family is to communicate effectively with your employer and your family. Let your employer know your priorities and your family commitments, so they can support you in achieving your goals. Likewise, communicate with your family and set expectations for your work commitments. This will help to reduce conflicts and ensure that everyone is on the same page.

It is also essential to take care of yourself to ensure that you are able to balance work and family effectively. This means prioritizing self-care activities such as exercise, meditation, or hobbies that help you to relax and recharge. Taking care of yourself will help you to be more productive and focused both at work and at home.

Finally, it is important to be flexible and adaptable when it comes to balancing work and family. There will be times when work demands more of your time, and other times when family demands more of your time. Being flexible and adaptable will help you to navigate these challenges and ensure that you are able to meet the needs of both your work and your family.

In conclusion, balancing work and family is a challenging but essential aspect of fatherhood. By establishing clear boundaries, communicating effectively, prioritizing self-care, and being flexible and adaptable, you can achieve a balance that allows you to fulfill your responsibilities both at work and at home.

LEGACY

Creating a meaningful legacy

As a father, you have a unique opportunity to create a lasting impact on the world through the legacy you leave behind. Your legacy is not just the material possessions you accumulate or the wealth you amass, but the values, beliefs, and principles you instill in your children and the people around you.

Creating a meaningful legacy requires a conscious effort to align your actions with your values and beliefs. It means being intentional about the kind of person you want to be and the kind of impact you want to have on the world.

The first step in creating a meaningful legacy is to define your values and beliefs. What do you stand for? What principles guide your actions? Take the time to reflect on these questions and write down your answers. This will serve as a compass for your actions and decisions.

Next, focus on the relationships that matter most to you. Your family and close friends are the ones who will be most affected by your legacy. Invest time and energy in nurturing these relationships and creating meaningful memories with them.

One of the most important aspects of creating a meaningful legacy is to be a positive influence on your children. Your children learn from your actions and behaviors, and they will carry these lessons with them for the rest of their lives. Be a role model for them by living out your values and beliefs and demonstrating integrity, kindness, and empathy.

Another way to create a meaningful legacy is to give back to your community. Make a difference in the lives of others by volunteering your time, donating to charity, or starting a community project. These acts of kindness will have a ripple effect that extends far beyond your own lifetime.

Finally, remember that creating a meaningful legacy is a lifelong process. It requires consistent effort and a commitment to personal growth and development. By living out your values and beliefs, nurturing your relationships, and making a positive impact on the world, you can leave a legacy that will inspire and impact future generations.

Passing on values and traditions

Passing on Values and Traditions

As fathers, one of our most important roles is to pass on our values and traditions to our children. This is not always an easy task, but it is essential if we want to raise children who will be successful, happy, and well-adjusted adults.

One of the first things we need to do is to identify our own values and traditions. What is important to us? What do we believe in? What are our family traditions? Once we have answered these questions, we can begin to think about how we can pass these values and traditions on to our children.

One way to do this is to lead by example. Children learn by watching and imitating their parents. If we want our children to value honesty, integrity, and hard work, we need to model these behaviors ourselves. We need to be the kind of person we want our children to be.

Another way to pass on our values and traditions is to talk to our children about them. We can share stories about our own childhood and the values and traditions that were important to us. We can explain why these things are important and why we want our children to carry them on.

We can also involve our children in our family traditions. Whether it's a holiday celebration, a family meal, or a special activity, we can make sure our children are a part of it. This will help them to feel connected to our family and our values.

Finally, we can encourage our children to develop their own values and traditions. We can support them in exploring their interests and passions and help them to develop their own sense of identity. This will help them to become independent adults who are grounded in their own values and traditions.

In conclusion, passing on our values and traditions is an important part of fatherhood. It requires us to be intentional about the kind of person we want to be and the kind of family we want to have. By leading by example, talking to our children, involving them in our traditions, and encouraging them to develop their own values, we can create a legacy that will last for generations to come.

Leaving a positive impact on your family

As a father, you have the potential to leave a significant impact on your family. Your actions, words, and behavior can shape your children's future, and it's essential to make a positive impression on them. Leaving a positive impact on your family requires a conscious effort to be mindful of your actions and to prioritize your family's well-being.

One of the most crucial aspects of leaving a positive impact on your family is being present. In today's busy world, it's easy to get caught up in work, hobbies, or other distractions, but being present with your family is key. Take the time to listen to your children, engage in conversations with them, and show them that you value their opinions and thoughts. By doing so, you create a sense of connection and belonging, which is essential for a healthy family dynamic.

Another way to leave a positive impact on your family is by modeling positive behavior. Children learn by example, and as a father, you are a role model for your children. Displaying positive qualities such as kindness, empathy, and respect will help your children develop these traits themselves. Additionally, showing your children how to handle adversity and challenges with resilience and a growth mindset will help them navigate life's challenges.

Communication is another key aspect of leaving a positive impact on your family. Effective communication involves active listening, expressing your thoughts and feelings clearly, and being open to feedback. Encouraging open communication within your family will create a safe space for everyone to express themselves and build trust.

Finally, prioritize spending quality time with your family. Whether it's going on a family vacation, playing games together, or simply having dinner together, spending time together creates memories and strengthens bonds. It's essential to create a healthy work-life balance and prioritize your family's time and needs.

In summary, leaving a positive impact on your family requires being present, modeling positive behavior, effective communication, and spending quality time together. By doing so, you create a strong family foundation that will benefit your children for years to come.

PUTTING IT ALL TOGETHER

Developing a personal action plan

Developing a Personal Action Plan

After identifying your goals and vision, the next step is to develop a personal action plan that will guide you towards achieving your desired outcomes. A personal action plan is a written document that outlines the steps you need to take to achieve your goals. It is a roadmap that helps you stay focused and motivated, and holds you accountable for your progress.

To develop an effective personal action plan, you need to follow these steps:

1. Identify your goals: Start by identifying your long-term and short-term goals. Your long-term goals are your ultimate objectives, while your short-term

goals are the stepping stones towards achieving your long-term goals. Write down your goals in a clear and specific manner.

2. Break down your goals: Once you have identified your goals, break them down into smaller, measurable tasks. This will help you stay motivated and make progress towards achieving your goals.

3. Create a timeline: Set realistic deadlines for each task. This will help you stay on track and avoid procrastination.

4. Prioritize your tasks: Identify the tasks that are most important and prioritize them. This will help you focus your time and energy on the tasks that will bring the most significant results.

5. Take action: Once you have developed your personal action plan, take action. Do not wait for the perfect moment or for everything to be perfect. Start working towards your goals today.

6. Monitor your progress: Regularly review your personal action plan and monitor your progress. Celebrate your successes and learn from your

failures. Use the feedback to adjust your plan and stay on track.

In conclusion, developing a personal action plan is crucial for achieving your goals and creating a mastery mindset for fatherhood. It helps you stay focused, motivated, and accountable for your progress. Remember to identify your goals, break them down, create a timeline, prioritize your tasks, take action, and monitor your progress. With a personal action plan, you can achieve greatness in fatherhood and create a lasting legacy for your family.

Implementing the Fatherhood Blueprint

Implementing the Fatherhood Blueprint

Now that you have a clear understanding of what the Fatherhood Blueprint is, it is time to put it into action. The Fatherhood Blueprint is not just a theory or an idea, it is a practical guide that can help you become a better father. Here are some tips on how to implement the Fatherhood Blueprint:

1. Set clear goals

The first step in implementing the Fatherhood Blueprint is to set clear goals. What do you want to achieve as a father? What kind of relationship do you want to have with your children? What values do you want to instill in them? Once you have set your goals, you can create a plan to achieve them.

2. Be present

Being present is one of the most important things you can do as a father. Your children need your attention, your time, and your love. Make sure you are there for them, both physically and emotionally. Put away your phone, turn off the TV, and give them your undivided attention.

3. Communicate effectively

Communication is key to any relationship, and your relationship with your children is no exception. Make sure you are communicating effectively with them. Listen to what they have to say, ask questions, and show empathy. Be open and honest with them, and encourage them to do the same with you.

4. Lead by example

As a father, you are a role model for your children. Lead by example and show them how to live a life of integrity, respect, and kindness. Model the behavior you want to see in them, and they will follow your lead.

5. Be flexible

Fatherhood is not a one-size-fits-all experience. Every child is different, and every situation is unique. Be flexible in your approach and adjust your parenting style as needed. Be willing to try new things and learn from your mistakes.

Implementing the Fatherhood Blueprint takes time and effort, but it is worth it. By following these tips, you can become a better father and create a strong, loving relationship with your children. Remember, the Fatherhood Blueprint is not a destination, it is a journey. Keep working at it, and you will see the results in your children's lives.

Measuring progress and success

Measuring Progress and Success

One of the essential aspects of fatherhood is setting goals and measuring progress. As a father, you have a vision of what kind of relationship you want to have with your children and what kind of impact you want to make on their lives. However, it's not enough to have a vision; you also need to have a plan and a way to measure your progress towards achieving your goals.

Measuring progress and success is a critical component of a mastery mindset for fatherhood. It's essential to have a way to track your progress and evaluate your performance so that you can make adjustments and keep moving forward.

Here are some tips for measuring progress and success as a father:

1. Set clear, specific goals

The first step in measuring progress is to set clear, specific goals. Your goals should be specific, measurable, achievable, relevant, and time-bound (SMART). Setting

SMART goals will give you a clear target to aim for and a way to measure your progress.

2. Keep a journal

Keeping a journal is an excellent way to track your progress and reflect on your experiences as a father. You can use your journal to write down your goals, track your progress, and reflect on your successes and challenges.

3. Get feedback from your children

Another way to measure your progress as a father is to get feedback from your children. Ask your children how they feel about your relationship and what you can do to improve. Getting feedback from your children will help you identify areas where you need to improve and areas where you are doing well.

4. Celebrate your successes

It's essential to celebrate your successes as a father. Celebrating your successes will give you a sense of accomplishment and motivate you to continue working towards your goals.

5. Be patient

Measuring progress and success takes time. It's essential to be patient and persistent in your efforts. Remember that progress is not always linear, and there will be setbacks and challenges along the way.

In conclusion, measuring progress and success is an essential component of a mastery mindset for fatherhood. Setting clear goals, keeping a journal, getting feedback from your children, celebrating your successes, and being patient are all essential strategies for measuring progress and achieving success as a father.

CONCLUSION

The importance of a Mastery Mindset for Fatherhood

The Importance of a Mastery Mindset for Fatherhood

Fatherhood is a journey that requires a lot of dedication and commitment. It is a role that demands you to be the best version of yourself, to provide guidance, support, and love for your children. However, being a good father is not something that comes naturally to everyone. It takes effort, patience, and a mastery mindset.

A mastery mindset is a state of mind that embraces challenges, embraces failures and learns from them, and continuously strives for self-improvement. It is a mindset that enables you to develop your skills and abilities to their fullest potential. When it comes to fatherhood, a mastery mindset is the key to success.

Here are some reasons why a mastery mindset is essential for fatherhood:

1. Self-improvement

A mastery mindset encourages self-improvement. As a father, you must always be willing to learn and grow. You can only provide the best guidance and support for your children if you are continuously improving yourself.

2. Handling challenges

Fatherhood comes with its own set of challenges. A mastery mindset enables you to handle these challenges with ease. It helps you to remain calm and composed in difficult situations, and to find solutions to problems.

3. Role-modeling

As a father, you are a role model for your children. Your behavior and actions have a significant impact on their lives. A mastery mindset enables you to set a good example for your children. It helps you to demonstrate the importance of hard work, dedication, and self-improvement.

4. Building relationships

Fatherhood is all about building relationships with your children. A mastery mindset enables you to build strong, positive relationships with your children. It helps you to communicate effectively, understand their needs, and be present for them.

In conclusion, a mastery mindset is crucial for fatherhood. It enables you to be the best version of yourself, to handle challenges with ease, to set a good example for your children, and to build strong relationships with them. By adopting a mastery mindset, you can become the best father you can be, and provide your children with the guidance, support, and love they need to thrive.

Reflection on the Fatherhood Blueprint

Reflection on the Fatherhood Blueprint

As fathers, we often find ourselves struggling to balance the responsibilities of work, family, and personal growth. We want to be good providers, loving partners, and role models for our children. However, we also want to pursue our passions, develop our skills, and achieve our goals. How can we reconcile these competing demands and create a fulfilling life as fathers?

The Fatherhood Blueprint provides a framework for mastering the challenges of fatherhood and achieving success in all areas of our lives. It combines the principles of personal development, leadership, and parenting to create a holistic approach to fatherhood. Let us reflect on these principles and how they can help us become better fathers.

Firstly, the Fatherhood Blueprint emphasizes the importance of self-awareness and self-mastery. We cannot lead our families effectively if we cannot lead ourselves. We need to develop a growth mindset, cultivate positive habits, and manage our emotions and thoughts. When we have a strong sense of self, we can model resilience, empathy, and confidence for our children.

Secondly, the Fatherhood Blueprint emphasizes the power of intention and purpose. We need to clarify our values, vision, and goals as fathers. We need to align our actions with our intentions and create a sense of meaning and direction in our lives. When we have a clear sense of purpose, we can inspire our children to find their own purpose and contribute to the world.

Thirdly, the Fatherhood Blueprint emphasizes the importance of relationships and communication. We need to cultivate strong connections with our partners, children, and community. We need to listen actively, communicate clearly, and resolve conflicts effectively. When we have healthy relationships, we can create a loving and supportive environment for our children to thrive.

Fourthly, the Fatherhood Blueprint emphasizes the value of growth and contribution. We need to continuously learn, improve, and give back to our families and society. We need to model lifelong learning, creativity, and generosity. When we have a growth mindset and a spirit of service, we can inspire our children to become lifelong learners and compassionate leaders.

In conclusion, the Fatherhood Blueprint offers a comprehensive and practical approach to fatherhood. It invites us to reflect on our values, vision, and goals as fathers, and to develop the mastery mindset that enables us to create a life of purpose, fulfillment, and impact. Let us embrace this blueprint and become the best fathers we can be.

Final Thoughts

As we come to the end of this book, I want to leave you with some final thoughts that I hope will serve as a reminder of the importance of a mastery mindset for fatherhood.

Firstly, I want to emphasize that fatherhood is not easy, but it is worth it. It requires patience, resilience, and a willingness to learn and grow. But the rewards of seeing your children grow and thrive are immeasurable.

Secondly, I want to encourage you to embrace the idea of mastery. Mastery is not about being perfect, but rather about striving to be the best version of yourself. It is about setting high standards for yourself and your children, and continually working towards achieving those goals.

Thirdly, I want to remind you that fatherhood is a journey, not a destination. There will be ups and downs, successes and failures, but it is important to stay committed to the process. Keep learning, keep growing, and keep striving to be the best father you can be.

Finally, I want to leave you with a quote from the great philosopher Aristotle. He said, "We are what we repeatedly do. Excellence, then, is not an act, but a habit." This quote perfectly sums up the idea of a mastery mindset. It is not about achieving perfection in one moment, but rather about consistently striving for excellence in everything you do.

In conclusion, I hope this book has inspired you to adopt a mastery mindset for fatherhood. Remember, you have the power to create the blueprint for your own success as a father. Embrace the journey, stay committed to the process, and strive for excellence in everything you do. Thank you for reading.

APPENDIX

Additional Resources

Additional Resources

As a father, you have the power to shape the lives of your children in ways that will impact them for years to come. But fatherhood is not always easy, and you may find yourself struggling to balance your responsibilities at work and at home, or feeling unsure about how to connect with your kids on a deeper level.

Fortunately, there are many resources available to help you navigate the challenges of fatherhood and develop a mastery mindset that will allow you to thrive as a parent. Here are just a few of the resources that you may find helpful:

1. Books and podcasts on fatherhood and parenting

There are many great books and podcasts out there that offer insights and advice on how to be a better father. Some of the most popular books on fatherhood include "The Art of Fatherhood" by David Hirsch, "Strong Fathers, Strong Daughters" by Meg Meeker, and "Fatherhood: Rising to the Ultimate Challenge" by Etan Thomas. Podcasts like "The Dad Edge" and "The Good Dad Project" also offer a wealth of information and inspiration for fathers.

2. Online communities and forums

Sometimes it can be helpful to connect with other fathers who are going through similar experiences. There are many online communities and forums where you can share your thoughts and questions with other dads. Some popular options include the "Dad's Group Inc." Facebook group, the "Daddy's Digest" forum, and the "Dads Who Lift" community.

3. Parenting classes and workshops

If you're looking for more structured support, consider taking a parenting class or attending a workshop. Many community centers and schools offer classes on topics like positive discipline, effective communication, and building strong family relationships. You may also find workshops specifically geared towards fathers, such as the "Boot Camp for New Dads" program.

4. Counseling and therapy

If you're struggling with issues like stress, anxiety, or depression, consider seeking out counseling or therapy. A mental health professional can help you explore your feelings and develop strategies for coping with the challenges of fatherhood. You may also consider family therapy if you're having difficulties with your partner or children.

Remember, being a father is a journey, and there will be times when you feel like you're not doing everything perfectly. But by taking advantage of these resources and developing a mastery mindset, you can become the best possible father for your children.

Worksheets and Exercises

Worksheets and Exercises

In this chapter, we will explore various worksheets and exercises that will help you develop a mastery mindset for fatherhood. These exercises are designed to help you reflect on your parenting philosophy, identify your strengths and weaknesses, and develop a plan to become a better father.

Worksheet 1: Reflection on Parenting Philosophy

This worksheet will help you reflect on your parenting philosophy. It is important to define your parenting philosophy because it will guide your parenting decisions and actions.

Instructions:

1. Take a few minutes to think about your parenting philosophy.

2. Write down your parenting philosophy in one or two sentences.

3. Reflect on your parenting philosophy and ask yourself the following questions:

- Does my parenting philosophy align with my values?

- Does my parenting philosophy reflect my parenting goals?

- Does my parenting philosophy support my child's development and well-being?

Worksheet 2: Identifying Strengths and Weaknesses

This worksheet will help you identify your strengths and weaknesses as a father. It is important to know your strengths and weaknesses so that you can focus on improving your weaknesses and leveraging your strengths.

Instructions:

1. Take a few minutes to think about your strengths and weaknesses as a father.
2. Write down your strengths and weaknesses in two separate columns.
3. Reflect on your strengths and weaknesses and ask yourself the following questions:

- How can I leverage my strengths to become a better father?
- What steps can I take to improve my weaknesses as a father?

Exercise 1: Daily Reflection

This exercise will help you reflect on your daily parenting experiences. It is important to reflect on your parenting experiences because it will help you learn from your mistakes and improve your parenting skills.

Appendix

Instructions:

1. At the end of each day, take a few minutes to reflect on your parenting experiences.
2. Ask yourself the following questions:

- What did I do well today as a father?
- What could I have done better today as a father?

1. Write down your reflections in a journal.

Exercise 2: Goal Setting

This exercise will help you set parenting goals. It is important to set parenting goals because it will help you focus on what is important and improve your parenting skills.

Instructions:

2. Take a few minutes to think about your parenting goals.
3. Write down your parenting goals in one or two sentences.
4. Reflect on your parenting goals and ask yourself the following questions:

- Are my parenting goals specific and measurable?

- Are my parenting goals realistic and achievable?
- Are my parenting goals aligned with my parenting philosophy and values?

In conclusion, these worksheets and exercises will help you develop a mastery mindset for fatherhood. By reflecting on your parenting philosophy, identifying your strengths and weaknesses, reflecting on your daily experiences, and setting parenting goals, you will become a better father and create a positive impact on your child's life.

GLOSSARY OF TERMS.

Glossary of Terms

As you embark on your journey to creating a mastery mindset for fatherhood, you may come across some terms that are unfamiliar to you. This glossary of terms is here to help you understand the terminology used in this book, as well as in the world of fatherhood and personal development.

Mastery Mindset: A state of mind where you believe that your abilities can be developed through dedication and hard work. This mindset allows you to embrace challenges, persist through obstacles, and learn from failures.

Fatherhood: The state of being a father or the role of a father in a family. Fatherhood involves providing emotional, financial, and physical support to your children.

Personal Development: The process of improving your skills, knowledge, and mindset to become a better version of yourself. Personal development involves setting goals, learning new things, and developing new habits.

Self-Awareness: The ability to understand your thoughts, emotions, and actions. Self-awareness allows you to identify your strengths and weaknesses, and make improvements to become a better person.

Emotional Intelligence: The ability to recognize and manage your emotions, as well as the emotions of others. Emotional intelligence involves empathy, self-awareness, and social skills.

Communication: The process of exchanging information, ideas, and emotions between individuals. Effective communication involves active listening, clarity, and empathy.

Boundaries: Limits that you set to protect your physical, emotional, and mental well-being. Boundaries allow you to establish healthy relationships and maintain your self-respect.

Resilience: The ability to bounce back from setbacks and adversity. Resilience involves having a positive mindset, seeking support, and learning from failures.

Time Management: The practice of organizing and prioritizing your time to achieve your goals. Effective time management involves setting priorities, avoiding distractions, and delegating tasks.

These are just a few of the many terms that you may encounter on your journey to creating a mastery mindset for fatherhood. By understanding these terms and incorporating them into your life, you can become a more effective and fulfilled father.

www.ingramcontent.com/pod-product-compliance
Lightning Source LLC
Chambersburg PA
CBHW032132090426
42743CB00007B/569